Galapagos

BOTH SIDES OF THE COIN

Pete Oxford & Graham Watkins

**Foreword by His Royal Highness,
Prince Philip, Duke of Edinburgh**

imagine!
New York
www.imaginebks.com

New York
www.imaginebks.com

Published by Imagine Publishing, Inc.
25 Whitman Road, Morganville, NJ 07751

Distributed in the United States by:
BookMasters Distribution Services, Inc.
30 Amberwood Parkway
Ashland, OH 44805

Distributed in Canada by:
BookMasters Distribution Services, Inc.
c/o Jacqueline Gross Associates
165 Dufferin Street
Toronto, Ontario, Canada M6K 3H6

Distributed in the United Kingdom by:
Publishers Group U.K., 8 The Arena, Mollison Avenue,
Enfield, EN3 7NL, U.K.

ISBN 13: 978-0-9822939-3-5
ISBN 10: 0-9822939-3-3
Library of Congress Control Number: 2009922012

Galapagos: Both Sides of the Coin
By Pete Oxford and Graham Watkins
E-mail: pete@peteoxford.com
www.peteoxford.com

Design: belénmena & Pete Oxford

For information about custom editions, special sales,
premium and corporate purchases, please contact Imagine
Publishing, Inc. at specialsales@imaginebks.com

BALMORAL CASTLE

The Galapagos Islands will always be associated with Charles Darwin and the development of his theory of the origin of species through a process of natural selection.

This year, 2009, happens to be the bicentenary of Charles Darwin's birth, and the 150th anniversary of the publication of On the Origin of Species. It also happens to be the 50th anniversary of the establishment of the Galapagos National Park and the Charles Darwin Foundation. The organizations were founded in recognition of the many unique natural features of these islands, which helped Darwin to develop his ideas, and to ensure that they were properly protected for future generations.

This book provides readers with a comprehensive photographic and written insight into the complex problems associated with the conservation of the very special ecosystem of the Galapagos Islands. It describes the remarkable achievements of the National Park and the Foundation, and the challenges they will face in the future.

**His Royal Highness, Prince Philip,
Duke of Edinburgh**

Inside front cover: The 1838 Ecuadorian eight escudo doubloon was the coin nailed to the mast by Capt. Ahab aboard his vessel the Pequod. It was offered as a reward to the sailor who first spotted the white whale, Moby Dick, in Herman Melville's novel. The story was developed from Melville's experiences in Galapagos.

6

Title page: An endemic Galapagos Penguin, *Spheniscus mendiculus*, glides through the water while hunting off Bartolomé Island.

Above: A pair of endemic Waved Albatross, *Phoebastria irrorata*, concentrates on its highly ritualized 'gamming' or courtship dance, the sequence of which seems to be unique to the pair involved and helps their mutual recognition after many months foraging alone at sea. Española Island.

Contents

A huge feeding flock, consisting of
thousands of Blue-footed Boobies,
Sula nebouxii excisa, gathers close to the
town of Puerto Villamil on Isabela Island.
Together they form a more efficient
feeding force as they plunge-dive in a
synchronized assault onto a large school of
bait fish swimming just below the surface.

9

Pete Oxford would like to dedicate this book to his wife, Reneé Bish, whose steadfast support of his photography is the backbone of their photographic team. Her dedication is without bounds.

Graham Watkins would like to dedicate this book to his parents, Colyn and Tonina, to whom he owes everything, including his interest in the natural world.

Together, both authors would like to dedicate *Galapagos: Both Sides of the Coin* to all Ecuadorians, especially those who live in Galapagos. They will determine the fate of these extraordinary islands.

"The natural history of these islands is eminently curious, and well deserves attention. Most of the organic productions are aboriginal creations, found nowhere else; there is even a difference between the inhabitants of the different islands; yet all show a marked relationship with those of America, though separated from that continent by an open space of ocean, between 500 and 600 miles in width. The archipelago is a little world within itself, or rather a satellite attached to America, whence it has derived a few stray colonists, and has received the general character of its indigenous productions. Considering the small size of these islands, we feel the more astonished at the number of their aboriginal beings, and at their confined range. Seeing every height crowned with its crater, and the boundaries of most of the lava-streams still distinct, we are led to believe that within a period, geologically recent, the unbroken ocean was here spread out. Hence, both in space and time, we seem to be brought somewhere near to that great fact—that mystery of mysteries—the first appearance of new beings on this earth."

Darwin, C.R., 1845, Journal of Researches into the Geology and Natural History of the Various Countries Visited by H.M.S.Beagle, Under the Command of Captain FitzRoy, R.N. from 1832 to 1836

11

An 1883 portrait of Charles Darwin, aged 74 years old, painted by John Collier.
Courtesy English Heritage Photo Library

12

A Galapagos Giant Tortoise, *Geochelone vandenburgi*, an animal which may weigh up to 250 kg, stares stoically at the photographer from the crater floor of Alcedo Volcano while steam billows from active vents behind.

14

A Lava Lizard, *Microlophus albermarlensis*, uses the head of a Marine Iguana, *Amblyrhynchus cristatus*, as a vantage point. It is noteworthy that here, at Cabo Douglas on the northwest of Fernandina, the Lava Lizards are brightly colored; whereas, at Punta Espinoza on the northeast, they are a uniform dark grey.

Prologue

The Galapagos Islands have inspired a range of emotions, from disgust to delight. William Dampier, in 1697, described the islands as "rocky, barren and hilly, producing neither tree, herb nor grass." Charles Darwin, in 1835, compared the landscape to the "cultivated parts of the infernal regions." Herman Melville, in 1837, described their "emphatic uninhabitableness." However, in 1924, William Beebe struggled in his writing to "reproduce some of the beauty and interest of these islands." Robert Bowman, in 1984, wrote, "No area on earth of comparable size has inspired more fundamental changes in Man's perspective of himself and his environment than the Galapagos Islands." In the pages that follow, we present the features of the Galapagos that gave rise to these fundamentally different perceptions.

In the first half of the book, we illustrate why the Galapagos archipelago is so important. We show you the charismatic wildlife, the geological features, the plant life, the endemic species, and the marine environment. We illustrate why the Galapagos National Park was included as one of the first four World Heritage Sites in 1978 and why, in 2001, the World Heritage Commission extended this recognition to the Galapagos Marine Reserve. Today, the Galapagos is one of the last well-conserved tropical archipelagos in the world, recognized globally for its role in guiding the thinking of Charles Darwin.

In the second half of the book, we look at conservation issues. We describe the human history of the archipelago. We discuss the present situation in the islands, focusing on the last twenty years. We end by presenting some of the possibilities for a sustainable future that will ensure the long-term conservation of these extraordinary islands.

While we do not pretend to have the answers for the complex conservation challenges of the Galapagos, we hope that this book will offer some suggestions about what we can do to ensure that the archipelago retains its magic. The islands have influenced the lives of many people; they have shaped the lives of some. The Galapagos have been a personal experience for both of us; they changed the course of our lives – and this book represents our written and photographic perspectives of the islands. Our greatest desire is that others experience what we have, and that these experiences serve as a call to action, inspiring the creation of a sustainable model for one of the world´s last remaining natural treasures, a model for sustainable societies everywhere.

16   Through a collaborative GNPS (Galapagos National Park Sevice) and CDRS (Charles Darwin Research Station) breeding program, a magnificent male Land Iguana, *Conolophus subcristatus*, previously reintroduced to its native Baltra Island, now once again roams wild where the species had become extinct.

A Great Blue Heron, *Ardea herodias*, frozen like a statue, patiently hunts the shoreline for prey. Santa Cruz Island.

Astonishing Galapagos

In 1987, Graham Watkins and I boarded a bus in La Libertad, on the Santa Elena peninsula of Ecuador, bound for Guayaquil to look for jobs as Galapagos naturalist guides. I had studied marine zoology at Bangor University in North Wales with Graham's brother, Andy, who, in 1982, had left for the exotic shores of Ecuador to work. Andy later told me about a job in aquaculture, and I followed him in 1985. Graham joined us a year later.

Over the horizon, the Galapagos Islands always had a major pull on both Graham and me, and after visiting as a tourist in late 1985, I had already sensed an inextricable link, destiny calling.

A tour company in Guayaquil offered to sponsor both of us through the 1987 guide-training course. Graham and I graduated first and second, respectively, in the class and immediately embarked on our new careers as licensed naturalist guides. Despite lousy pay and long tours of duty – 90 days on and 30 days off – the job was a dream come true. Like sponges, we soaked up everything written about the Galapagos and every evening we talked with other guides about the day's sightings. We became very familiar with the Galapagos and delighted in sharing our knowledge with visitors to excite and enthuse them with our passion for the islands. We wanted them to understand the intricacies of natural history, human aspects, problems, and pressures, as well as potential solutions, and to take these messages home with them. More than two decades later, we are still at it, and these pages go some way toward condensing our thoughts and feelings about the islands as we see them today.

Things have changed drastically since 1985. In those days, there were a few municipal trucks, some buses, an old Land Rover, some motorbikes, and a few other vehicles plying dirt roads. Fuel was stored in 55-gallon drums and money kept under mattresses. Today, the roads are a paved network through the inhabited islands, and there are traffic lights in Baquerizo Moreno and traffic jams in Puerto Ayora. Several hundred taxis cruise the streets, there are banks and a gas station, and 4-wheel drive vehicles abound. The focus has wandered, the passion for the islands seems lost, and money is the driving force. There is a huge disconnect and a failure to understand that every dollar spent in night clubs, bars, taxis, souvenir shops, grocery stores, and even in the hardware stores, comes, in one way or another, from the health and sanctity of the natural resources in the Galapagos. The iguanas, tortoises, boobies, and penguins, rather than the Bloody Marys and Cuba Libres, are the attractions for the thousands of tourists that arrive each year.

Having said that, the Galapagos archipelago remains extraordinary, indeed the visitor sites have changed little since our first sojourns to them more than two decades ago. Actually, the islands are better conserved today than they were 100 years ago.

For most visitors, the Galapagos Islands are that once-in-a-lifetime destination. In most cases, after dealing with the initial shock produced by the sight of large towns in the islands, the enchantment of the archipelago leaves them awestruck. They walk amongst masses of recumbent marine iguanas that are like miniature dragons blending into a lava background. They sit alongside oblivious Blue-footed Boobies as a male stretches, everything pointed in earnest towards the sky, whistling a plaintive note, almost begging to be noticed by the female. They witness the slow lumbering of a gigantic tortoise – a modern-day dinosaur – and watch playful sea lions swim circles around them and make eye contact with their intelligent gaze.

All of these experiences are extraordinary in the larger scheme of things. To pry yourself from the pull of the city and sit in tranquility under the glitter of more stars than you can imagine in the darkness of night – this is an encounter that touches the soul. Yet all of these things are commonplace, everyday occurrences in the Galapagos. We are privileged; Graham and I have each spent the best part of five years of our lives in and around the islands since our initial encounter, he as a naturalist guide and the director of the Charles Darwin Foundation, and I as a naturalist guide, tour leader, and, finally, photographer. We have also witnessed other extraordinary events. We have watched as great flows of incandescent volcanic rocks spew from parasitic cones to reach the sea and make it boil in a primordial display of nature's power. We have seen squadrons of hundreds of hammerhead sharks cruise by in a seemingly endless curtain of elasmobranch power. We have watched a captive-reared tortoise, folded into a sphere tight within its shell, finally struggle out of its confines, using its temporary little egg tooth to break free, and take its first breath of outside air. We have watched a Vampire Finch peck the elbow of a Nazca Booby until it bleeds and then drink its blood. We have also watched thousands of Blue-footed Boobies wheeling overhead until, on the command of a solitary shrill whistle, they react like a single organism and veer sharply, plunging to attack a school of fish below the surface.

In the making of this book, with special park permissions, I have camped at the bottom of a huge volcanic crater and been kept awake at night by the sounds of tortoise flatulence in the wallows close by. I have helped scientists in myriad ways, from capturing rare and endemic Galapagos Hawks to attaching satellite transmitters on Waved Albatross and hammerhead sharks. I have gone free-diving with a Whale Shark to attach an acoustic transmitter and have traveled the extent of the Galapagos cormorant and penguin colonies to help in the population census. The more I have seen, the more I want to see, and the more deeply I appreciate how special the islands are.

This book is something Reneé, my wife, and I have long wanted to publish – something more than a simple catalogue of wildlife images. At the risk of being a less commercial product, the idea of the book has been to highlight some of both the issues and the achievements, as well as to look at the reality of the modern-day Galapagos. Our overall aim is that, through better understanding of the islands, we will be better equipped to preserve them. As we look into what the future might bring, we hope to offer a view of potential paths the islands could take in the sincere hope that reason will prevail and that the Galapagos will retain the sense of magic, wildness, and mystery for which, since Darwin's days, the archipelago has become famous.

*"For in the end, we will conserve only what we love. We will love only what we understand.
We will understand only what we are taught."*   *Baba Dioum*

Pete Oxford, Santa Cruz. 2008

19

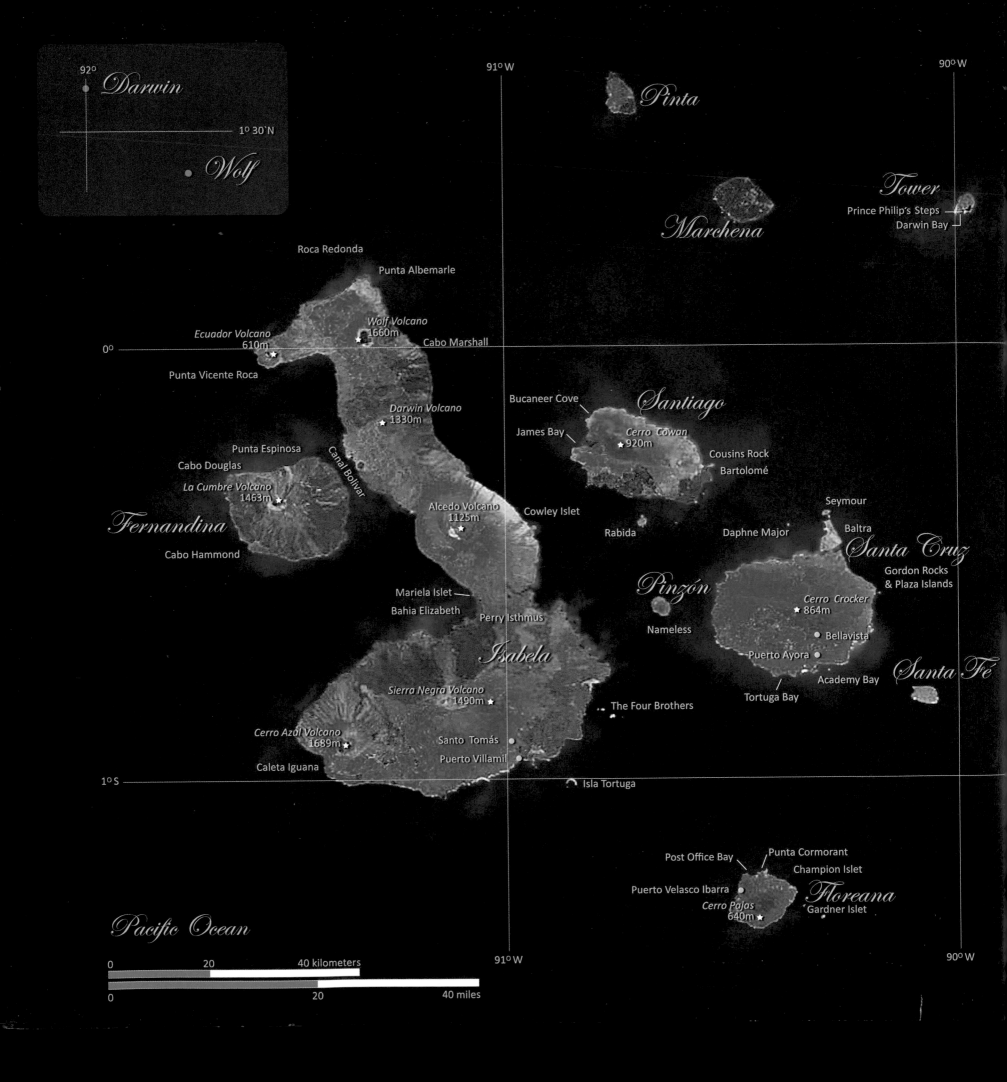

Darwin

92°

1° 30'N

Wolf

Pinta

Tower

Marchena

Prince Philip's Steps
Darwin Bay

91° W

90° W

Roca Redonda

Punta Albemarle

Ecuador Volcano
610m

Wolf Volcano
1660m

Cabo Marshall

0°

Punta Vicente Roca

Darwin Volcano
1330m

Bucaneer Cove

Santiago

James Bay

Cerro Cowan
920m

Cousins Rock

Bartolomé

Punta Espinosa

Cabo Douglas

Canal Bolívar

La Cumbre Volcano
1463m

Alcedo Volcano
1125m

Cowley Islet

Fernandina

Rabida

Daphne Major

Seymour

Baltra

Santa Cruz

Cabo Hammond

Gordon Rocks
& Plaza Islands

Pinzón

Cerro Crocker
864m

Mariela Islet

Bahia Elizabeth

Perry Isthmus

Nameless

Bellavista

Puerto Ayora

Santa Fé

Isabela

Academy Bay

Sierra Negra Volcano
1490m

The Four Brothers

Tortuga Bay

Cerro Azul Volcano
1689m

Santo Tomás

Puerto Villamil

Caleta Iguana

1° S

Isla Tortuga

Post Office Bay

Punta Cormorant

Champion Islet

Puerto Velasco Ibarra

Floreana

Pacific Ocean

Cerro Pajas
640m

Gardner Islet

0   20   40 kilometers

0   20   40 miles

91° W

90° W

0°

N

W ★ E

S

Pacific Ocean

Punta Pitt

Stephen's Bay

Kicker Rock

San Cristóbal

Puerto
Baquerizo   *Cerro San Joaquín*
Moreno ■   ★ 896m

● El Progreso

1° S

21

Gardner Bay

Punta
Suarez   *Española*
        ★ 220m

└ Punta Cevallos

A satellite map of Galapagos.
Note that the positions of Darwin and Wolf Islands are more
than 93.2 mi (150 km) to the northwest of nothern Isabela.

A mother Galapagos Sea Lion, *Zalophus wollebacki*, bonds with her offspring. The females usually pup once a year and the young Sea Lions will suckle and stay with their mothers as long as possible – until they are finally shunned and thus told to leave when the next generation arrives. Española Island.

> *"The natural history of this archipelago is very remarkable: it seems to be a little world within itself."*
>
> *Darwin, C.R., 1839, Journal of Researches*

The Galapagos Archipelago consists of 13 main islands and over 110 smaller islands and islets covering a land area of almost 4,971 square miles (8,000 square kilometers). They lie 621.4 miles (1,000 kilometers) from the Ecuadorian mainland, isolated by an expanse of ocean. Remoteness is the key to the extraordinary Galapagos wildlife as time and isolation have allowed the evolution of new species. Visitors readily identify with the eclectic group of creatures, including tropical species such as corals, reef fish, iguanas, mangroves, and hammerhead sharks, readily mixing with organisms associated with lower latitudes, such as macro-algae, penguins, albatross, and fur seals.

We present here the iconic species that are the "face" of the Galapagos. These species feature in the paintings, films, and millions of photographs taken every year. They have arrived from different points of the compass, but mainly from the South American continent, and some have evolved into new species. The survival of these species depends on the health of the marine and terrestrial ecosystems. The Galapagos Islands are unique and we begin this book by presenting the more familiar species that make up this extraordinary "little world within itself."

Above: A Blue-footed Booby male dances the 'Booby-two-step', showing off his bright blue feet in an attempt to attract a potential mate. Española Island.

Right: A Blue-footed Booby in the main nesting area at Punta Suarez, Española Island.

A baby Bottlenose Dolphin,
Tursiops truncatus, remains
close to its mother after having
just suckled. Wolf Island.

A young Galapagos Sea Lion takes to
the air while playing with a cohort off
Gardner Beach, Española Island.

Above: Marine Iguana. Santiago Island.

Right: Giant Tortoise. Alcedo, Isabela Island.

Opposite left: Galapagos Penguin. Isabela Island.

Opposite right: Bull Galapagos Fur Seal,
Arctocephalus galapagoensis. Cabo Douglas,
Fernandina Island.

Above: Sea Lion covered in sand.
Española Island.
Right: Giant Tortoise on the rim of
Alcedo Volcano, Isabela Island.

Efficient hunters, Sea Lions are able
to spend a large part of their day at
play or asleep. Española Island.

A Giant Tortoise enjoys a wallow that
helps it to keep cool (or warm up),
as well as reduce the nuisance of
biting insects. Santa Cruz Island.

A Galapagos Shark, *Carcharhinus galapagensis*. Wolf Island.

While flying in and landing close to a prospective mate or display area, a Blue-footed Booby makes a great show of his bright blue feet. Española Island.

Above: A Marine Iguana enjoys an elevated basking position. Puerto Ayora, Santa Cruz Island.

Right: Marine Iguanas bask in the sun, *en-masse,* to warm up sufficiently before entering the frigid waters of Cabo Douglas, in order to feed underwater on marine algae. Fernandina Island.

Rivers of incandescent molten lava
reached the sea and made it boil during
an eruption of a parasitic cone of *La
Cumbre* Volcano at Cabo Hammond,
Fernandina Island, in 1995.

The view of the steep-sided inside wall of
Alcedo crater on Isabela Island.

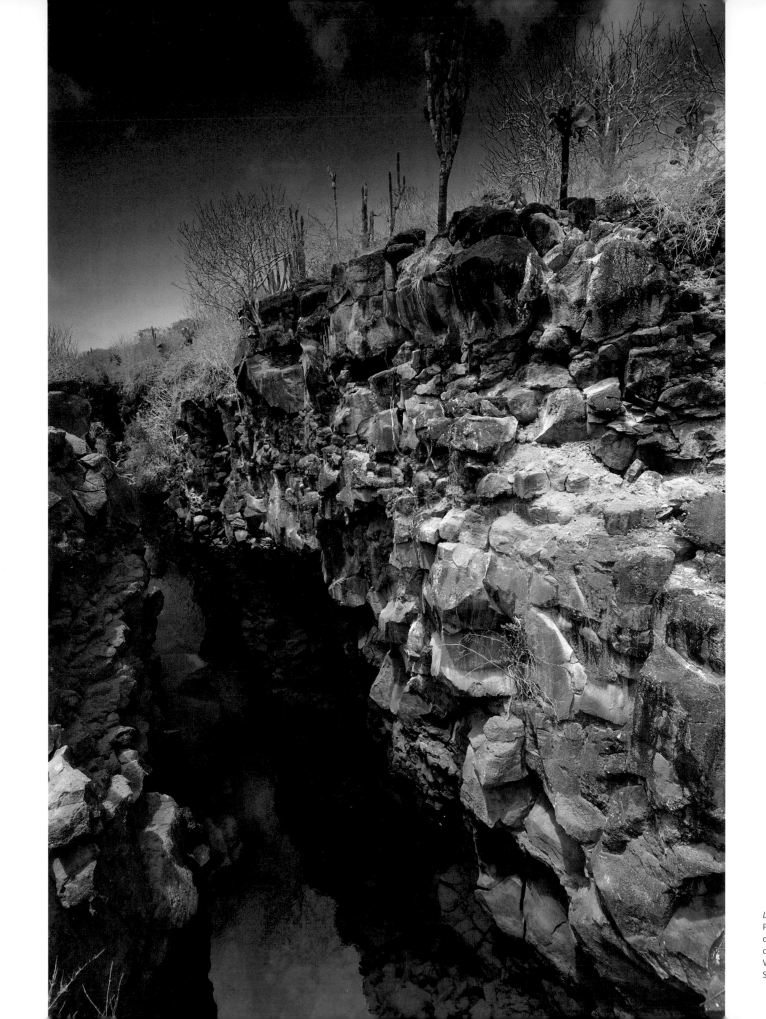

42

Las Grietas, eroded lava cracks in Puerto Ayora, is a favorite tourist destination where, with luck, one can enjoy snorkeling with White-tip Reef Sharks. Santa Cruz Island.

During cooling, cracks appear in lava and then gradually widen, mainly due to water erosion. These apertures form perfect collection traps for windblown hummus and detritus which, in turn, form an ideal substrate in a protected refuge for hardy plants to begin colonization of the lava. Santiago Island.

Pinnacle Rock, on Bartolomé
Island, is a famous example of an
eroded tuff cone.

During a volcanic eruption, the island of Fernandina gains both life and size, extending seaward as the hot lava is cooled by the sea.

The Lava Cactus, *Brachycereus nesioticus*, is an important pioneer plant of bare lava and its presence is an important first step in the creation of soil. Santiago Island.

Kicker Rock, also known as *León Dormido*, is a magnificent example of an eroded tuff cone. (Tuff is a soft rock formed of coalesced ash.) It lies off San Cristóbal Island, close to the capital, Puerto Baquerizo Moreno.

A close-up view of sulphur crystals.
Sierra Negra Volcano, Isabela Island.

Noxious gases, including hydrogen sulphide and sulphuric acid, billow up from an active sulphur fumarole on Sierra Negra Volcano, Isabela Island.

An eroded tuff cone, known as Darwin's
Arch, stands like a portal to Darwin
Island, a mecca for sub-aqua diving.

One of the classic Galapagos vistas, Pinnacle Rock, Bartolomé, with Santiago Island in the background. On Santiago can be seen the differences in age between the older, redder lava and the more recent black lava flow.

52

Red-hot lava pours from a miniature lava tube in the making. Cabo Hammond, Fernandina Island.

Galapagos has some of the largest and most extensive lava tubes in the world. As lava flows, the surface in contact with the air cools to form a crust, thus insulating the hot lava below. As the river of lava continues flowing, the crust thickens and hardens until it is solid. Eventually, the eruption stops and all the hot lava simply flows out under the crust, leaving a hollow tube. Santa Cruz Island.

Above and right: It was surprising to find tortoises traversing the hot, soft, sulphury mud on the fumaroles of Alcedo Volcano; however, they appear to benefit from intake of the minerals. Isabela Island.

A tiny rainbow highlights some of
the lush vegetation growth on the
inside of Sierra Negra Volcano,
Isabela Island.

"At an elevation of 1200 feet, and upwards, the land receives the moisture condensed from the clouds, which are drifted by the trade wind over this part of the ocean at an inconsiderable height. In consequence of this, the upper and central part of each island supports

a green and thriving vegetation..."

Darwin, C.R., 1838, Geographical Introduction to Mammalia, Zoology of the Voyage

Plants were among the first life forms to colonize the inhospitable surfaces of the Galapagos. Plants arrived attached to, or in the stomachs of, birds, as well as by wind or by rafting on the sea. However, arriving is not enough: once here, they need to establish and reproduce in a hostile environment. The first plants had to eke out an existence from whatever nutrients and water might have been available on baking volcanic substrates. A successful plant introduction every 8,000 to 10,000 years would have been sufficient to produce the vegetation we see today. One can envisage the process of arrival and establishment of plants and animals on volcanic landscapes by comparing the inhabitants of the newer western islands to those of the older eastern islands.

Plants have now clothed the older islands. Vegetation extends from the littoral zone of mangroves and other salt resistant plants, through the semi-arid zones forested by Palo Santo, *Bursera graveolens*, cacti, and other water constrained deciduous plants, through the transition zones of guayabillo, *Psidium galapageium*, and pega pega, *Pisonia floribunda*, to the humid zone of Scalesia and cat's claw, *Xanthoxylum fagara*, forests, Miconia, and ferns. Throughout the islands, the prevailing southeastern winds leave precipitation on the higher southern slopes. Altitudinal changes in temperature and rainfall are therefore the major determinants of different plant zones. These factors combine to produce the "green and thriving vegetation" that Darwin found.

Above: Detail of the endemic Galapagos Cotton flower, *Gossypium darwinii*. Santa Cruz Island.

Below: A Yellow Warbler, *Dendroica petechia aureola*, sings atop a *Muyuyu* shrub, *Cordia lutea*. Santa Cruz Island.

Right: A familiar scene to many visitors to Galapagos: two tree-like Giant Prickly Pear Cactus, *Opuntia echios var. echios*, tower above a dense red mat of Galapagos Carpetweed, *Sesuvium edmonstonei*, in the Arid Zone on South Plaza Island.

Salt-tolerant White Mangrove, *Laguncularia racemosa*, thrives on the coast near Puerto Villamil, Isabela Island. Galapagos has four species of mangrove, none of them endemic. This is due to their high threshold of long-distance dispersal, through floating seeds, which enhances genetic mixing.

In the Humid Zone in the highlands of Santa Cruz, the vegetation becomes lush and very dense – quite different from the Arid Zone where most of the visitor sites are to be found. Galapagos has 90 species of ferns, 90 species of moss and 110 species of liverworts, as well as a multitude of sedges, grasses, shrubs and trees.

A juvenile Yellow-crowned Night
Heron, *Nyctanassa violacea*, stands
in a tidal pool surrounded by Red
Mangrove and Prickly Pear Cactus.
Tower Island.

A Greater Flamingo, *Phoenicopterus ruber*, feeds in the shallows against a backdrop of large mangrove trees. *Cerro Dragon*, Santa Cruz Island.

Giant Prickly Pear Cactus trees on a small islet
off Santiago Island. With no rats on the island,
it is a favorite nesting site of Galapagos
Penguins, one of which can be seen on the left.

A view over the densely vegetated area
of Espumilla Beach on Santiago Island.

Above: Detail of Miconia.
Santa Cruz Island.

Right: The Miconia Zone is one of the
characteristic vegetation zones of the
highlands of Santa Cruz. With efforts by
the park wardens to eradicate some of
the aggressive, invasive plant species, the
Miconia is beginning to make a comeback
in certain places. Santa Cruz Island.

A dense stand of *Palo Santo* trees, *Bursera graveolens*. They are also known as Holy Stick trees as their wood, being a relative of Frankincense, is fragrant and burnt in churches. Floreana Island.

In stark contrast, the *Palo Santo* trees in the Arid Zone of Floreana look dead. They survive with no leaves most of the year in order to reduce water loss and only grow them again during the rainy season. Floreana Island.

Left: Fruit of the Button Mangrove,
Conocarpus erectus. Santa Cruz Island.

Center: Miconia flower, *Miconia
robinsoniana*. Santa Cruz Island.

Right: Fruit of Momordica, *Momordica
charantia*. Santa Cruz Island.

Top: Galapagos Passion Flower, *Passiflora foetida galapagensis*. Santa Cruz Island.

Center: White-haired Tournefortia, *Tournefortia pubescens*. Santa Cruz Island.

Bottom: Open fruit of Momordica, *Momordica charantia*. Santa Cruz Island.

The trees on the slightly elevated parts of many of the islands are often festooned with a moss-like liverwort known as 'Old Man's Beard'. Santa Cruz Island.

A Large Candelabra Cactus, *Jasminocereus thouarsii var. sclerocarpus*, grows out of bare lava on the west of Isabela.

The endemic Lava Gull, *Larus fuliginosus*, is possibly the
least numerous gull species in the world. It is, however,
found throughout the archipelago, often around human
settlements, being primarily a scavenger by trade. It
often breaks into a series of raucous 'laughs', showing
off its bright orange throat lining. Isabela Island.

*"Reviewing the facts here given, one is astonished at the amount of **creative force**, if such an expression may be used, displayed on these small, barren, and rocky islands…"*

Darwin, C.R., 1845, Journal of Researches

A key characteristic of the Galapagos is the number of "endemic" species – those found here and nowhere else. These endemic species are similar to, but differ sufficiently from, their mainland relatives in a way that is consistent with Darwin's theories. Almost all of the reptiles, 90% of the mammals, over 80% of the land birds, 30% of the plants, and an estimated 50% of the invertebrates are endemic. In the face of this extraordinary endemic diversity, one cannot help but read a little irony into Darwin's use of the term "creative force" with reference to the Galapagos.

The endemic reptiles include the tortoises, iguanas, lava lizards, geckos, and snakes. There are endemic mammals in the Galapagos, including rice rats. There is also a wide range of endemic land birds, including the finches, and there are several endemic marine birds, such as the Galapagos Penguin, the Flightless Cormorant, the Lava Gull, and the Swallow-tailed Gull. The flora of Galapagos includes some 180 endemic species. There are also endemic land snails, moths, and butterflies. Many of these species have small populations, often less than 1,000 individuals, making them highly vulnerable, and some of the smaller species may have already become extinct before scientists were able to record them.

The endemic Galapagos Flightless Cormorant, *Nannopterum harrisi*, is the largest of the 29 species of cormorant in the world and the only one that is flightless. Its dull plumage is set off by its bright turquoise eyes. Isabela Island.

An endemic Waved Albatross carefully preens the 'wavy' feathers on its chest that lend it its name. Española Island.

A bull Galapagos Fur Seal, above and right. These are the smallest of the world's fur seal species with an adult bull weighing only up to 142 lbs (64 kg). They are mostly nocturnal feeders, preying principally on fish and squid. Cabo Douglas, Fernandina Island.

Top: An endemic Galapagos Penguin floats at the surface in water reflecting the last rays of the sun on the cliffs at Tagus Cove. Isabela Island.

Bottom: A juvenile Striated Heron, *Butorides striatus*, feeds on an endemic Painted Locust, *Schistocerca melanocera*, on Santiago Island.

An endemic Waved Albatross flies
on outstretched wings designed
for extended periods of effortless
gliding. Española Island.

A young Galapagos Flightless Cormorant begs for food from its parent. Fernandina Island.

Having fortified their pair bond through a complicated dance, a pair of Waved Albatross relax at their nest. Española Island.

The small, endemic Galapagos Dove,
Zenaida galapagoensis, is the only
native species of the pigeon family
in the islands. It is widespread
throughout the archipelago and
apparently unafraid of humans.
Santa Cruz Island.

Portrait of a Marine Iguana.
Santa Cruz Island.

86 A Waved Albatross chick, above, starts life off as something of an 'ugly duckling', but soon develops into an exquisite adult bird, right. Española Island.

Above: Giant Tortoise and bones. Alcedo Volcano, Isabela Island.

Left: An estimated 15,000 Giant Tortoises roam wild in the Galapagos Islands, where they are the dominant natural herbivore. Their appearance takes one back to the Jurassic Age, when reptiles were at the apex of evolution.

Galapagos Fur Seal bull.
Santiago Island.

An endemic Galapagos Hawk, *Buteo galapagoensis*, one of the rarest non-threatened raptors in the world. Santa Fe Island.

Blue-footed Boobies plunge-dive onto
bait fish below. An endemic subspecies in
Galapagos, they have stereoscopic vision,
shielded nostrils, to prevent two jets of
water hitting the brain, and a spongy,
shock-absorbing tissue around the head
and breast. Isabela Island.

The Brown Pelican, *Pelecanus occidentalis urinator*, an endemic subspecies to the Galapagos, like the Blue-footed Booby, is also a plunge–diver; however, pelicans lack the grace of boobies, having a much more awkward diving technique. Here it is seen scratching its throat pouch while the protective nictitating membrane covers the eye. Santa Cruz Island.

A Swallow-tailed Gull flies in to join
its mate. Española Island.

A pair of endemic Swallow-tailed Gulls, *Larus furcatus*, said to be the most beautiful gull in the world and the only one that is nocturnal. They feed mostly on squid. Tower Island.

Left: An unfledged baby Galapagos Penguin at the entrance to its nest burrow. Mariela Islet, Isabela Island.

Center: Swallow-tailed Gull chick. Punta Cevallos, Española Island.

Right: A Galapagos Sea Lion pup. Fernandina Island.

A mother and new born Galapagos Fur Seal.
The pup is less than half an hour old. Cabo
Douglas, Fernandina Island.

A breeding pair of Galapagos
Flightless Cormorants and Lava
Cactus. Isabela Island.

A bull Galapagos Fur Seal surrounded
by Marine Iguanas. Fernandina Island.

100

The endemic Galapagos Flycatcher,
Myriarchus magnirostris, a very tame
bird that is widespread throughout the
islands. Santa Cruz Island.

The endemic Galapagos Cotton, the showiest and largest of all native blooms in the islands. The seeds are important as a food source, while the cotton it produces is used by certain birds to line their nests. Santa Cruz Island.

Swallow-tailed gulls feed at night, mostly on fish and squid, flying tens of miles out to sea and possibly using the prey's own bioluminescence to help detect them. The bright red eye-ring around the eye is thought to improve night vision and in addition, the gulls may employ a rudimentary form of echo-location. Back at the nest, the chick pecks at the white base and tip of the bill to stimulate the parent to regurgitate food. White is more visible to the chick at night, compared to the red bill-tip of most other gulls—red being the first wave-length lost in darkness. Española Island.

An unsure Sea Lion gives the taller albatross a wide berth on the beach at Punta Cevallos, Española Island.

A Marine Iguana and Sally Lightfoot Crab,
Grapsus grapsus. Fernandina Island.

"There is grandeur in this view of life. . . .that, whilst this planet has gone cycling on according to the fixed law of gravity, from so simple a beginning endless forms most beautiful and most wonderful have been, and are being, evolved."

Darwin, C.R., 1859, On the Origin of Species by Means of Natural Selection

Taxonomic disharmony and adaptive radiation are important characteristics of the Galapagos.

The complete absence of some groups of species, or taxonomic disharmony, is a striking characteristic of the Galapagos. Disharmony exists because it is difficult for some species not only to arrive but also to establish in the islands. For example, there are no native amphibians in the islands, because it is practically impossible for them to cross the 600 miles (1,000 km) of sea – despite mainland Ecuador being one of the richest areas for amphibians in the world. Likewise, there are few orchids and no hummingbirds in the Galapagos, despite mainland Ecuador having more species of these two groups than any other country in the world.

As one moves from island to island, one finds subtle differences among what, otherwise, look like the same species. Take, for example, the Giant Tortoises, which differ from island to Island and even from volcano to volcano on Isabela Island. The same is true of many other organisms, including mockingbirds, finches, lizards, snakes, and snails, as well as Opuntia, Scalesia, and 16 other genera of vascular plants. These differences result from adaptive radiation, the process wherein populations occupy vacant niches and become reproductively isolated from ancestral stock, eventually evolving into separate species. These vacant niches exist partly because of taxonomic disharmony. The differences from island to island, coupled with similarities with mainland species, helped initiate Darwin's thinking about how species originate.

Since Darwin's times, we have generated a much deeper understanding of the processes of isolation, natural selection, and speciation that underlie evolution, though there is still much work to do to comprehend fully the formation of the "endless forms" of the Galapagos.

A good example of speciation within the archipelago is the case of the iguanas. Both the Marine and the Land Iguana are thought to have evolved from a common ancestor, such as the Green Iguana, *Iguana iguana* which could have arrived by rafting. However, further division occurs within the land iguanas, whereby the species *Conolophus subcristatus* (left) is widespread throughout the archipelago, while a second evolved species, *Conolophus pallidus* (right), is restricted to Santa Fe Island.

110 A female Blue-footed Booby.
Her darkly stained iris gives the
impression of a larger pupil than
the male. North Seymour Island.

An endemic Nazca Booby, *Sula granti*, remains alert while studying the photographer from its position of rest. Tower Island.

111

Left: A 'modern' Medium Ground Finch, *Geospiza fortis*, using all-weather, non-biodegradable plastic in its nest construction, nestled amongst some cactus pads a meter from a park bench at the public dock. Note that the Darwin's finches add a roof to their nests to protect them from the equatorial sun. Puerto Ayora, Santa Cruz Island.

112

Right: A Galapagos Painted Locust warms up in the early morning, facing the sun while clinging to an Opuntia Cactus pad. Santa Cruz Island.

Top: An adult Sally Lightfoot Crab, conspicuous and ubiquitous around the archipelago, adds a splash of color to the shoreline. San Cristóbal Island.

Bottom: An adult Ghost Crab, *Ocypode gaudichaudii*, also widespread on the sandy beaches of the island. They are shy and duck down into their burrows many meters ahead of someone walking along the beach. These crabs are the culprits that leave the tiny balls of sand of the beach. When out and about, their stalked eyes stand vertically, giving a somewhat surprised attitude. When in their burrows, they lie flat in special grooves. Santiago Island.

114 One of the most famous examples of adaptive radiation is found among the Darwin's finches where, from a small errant founder colony, thirteen species have evolved to fill vacant niches normally occupied by other groups in a more biodiverse habitat.

Right: Darwin's finch beaks have specialized to best suit their function. The Cactus Finch, *Geospiza scandens*, at left, has a long, down-curved beak for feeding on opuntia seeds, while the Woodpecker Finch, *Cactospiza pallidus*, right, has a strong, stout beak, which it uses (often employing a twig as a tool) in the fashion of a woodpecker to dig insect grubs out of the rotten wood.

Left: The smallest of the finches, also with the most diminutive, tweezer-like, beak, is the Warbler Finch, *Certhidea olivacea*. It is very warbler-like, to the extent that it is the only one of Darwin's finches with any real song. It searches under leaves for small insects.

Right: By comparison the largest of the ground finches, the Large Ground Finch, *Geospiza magnirostris*, has a hugely powerful beak with which it is able to crack open large and hard seeds unavailable to the other finches.

There is huge variation between the coloration
of the Lava Lizards throughout the archipelago.
This displaying male from Santa Cruz,
Microlophus albemarlensis, shows a lot of
varied color and patterning, whereas those
of the same species on Punta Espinoza on
Fernandina, which live on black lava, are
themselves almost totally black.

Female Lava Lizards show varying degrees of red on their throats as adults. As is the case with the Marine Iguanas, the reddest of all are those found on Española Island, as illustrated above. *Microlophus delanonis*.

Red-footed Boobies, *Sula sula websteri*, the smallest of the Galapagos boobies, live on the extremities of the islands, from where they range far out to sea to feed. I have often seen them deftly catching flying fish on the 'wing'. Throughout the red-footed boobies' pan-tropical distribution, the birds exhibit a typical color morph of 90% white and 10% brown; whereas, only 10% of the Galapagos population exhibits a white morph. Wolf Island.

"What! A white one?"
The more common brown morph of
the Red-footed Booby is seen perching
in the Red Mangrove on Tower Island.
The Red-foots are the only Galapagos
boobies with prehensile feet, allowing
them to perch successfully.

There are fifteen species and six subspecies of the endemic *Scalesia genus* that have evolved in the Galapagos, making them one of the best examples of adaptive radiation in the islands. They range from small shrubs to 50 foot (15 meter) tall trees forming dense forests. They are members of the familiar daisy family.

Top: Radiate-headed Scalesia, *Scalesia affinis*. Isabela Island.

Bottom: Heller's Scalesia, *Scalesia helleri*. Santa Cruz Island.

A caterpillar of a sphinx moth, *Erinnyis ello encantada*, is seen here, for the first time, using Button Mangrove, *Conocarpus erectus,* as a host plant. Puerto Ayora, Santa Cruz Island.

Top: A Red-billed Tropicbird, *Phaethon aethereus*, incubates its single egg in a crevice on Española Island.

Bottom: An American Oystercatcher, *Haematopus palliates*, flees the incoming surf carrying a mole crab that it has just extracted from the soft sand. Santiago Island.

Once common on Santa Cruz Island, the Vermillion Flycatcher, *Pyrocephalus rubinus*, is becoming increasingly difficult to encounter. The male is an unmistakable vermillion red, while the female is a dull yellow. Like many flycatchers, they sally from a favorite perch to catch insects on the wing. Santo Tomás, Isabela Island.

Due to the geographic isolation of various populations of species around the island, a gradual divergence and evolution is taking place before our very eyes. One example is the Marine Iguana populations which, on most islands, are a fairly uniform, lava gray. On Española (right), the males, especially, take on a very colorful hue, particularly in the breeding season. Santa Cruz Island.

A male Marine Iguana in breeding condition.
Española Island.

An endemic subspecies of the Green
Turtle, *Chelonia mydas agassisi*, swims
inquisitively towards the photographer.
Cousins Rock.

"The Bay swarmed with animals; Fish, Shark & Turtles were popping their heads up in all parts."

Darwin, C.R., 1835, Beagle Diary

In the 1920s, William Beebe was the first person to explore the underwater marine environment of the Galapagos. The seas around the islands are as diverse as are the terrestrial environments. Three distinct currents create different temperature and nutrient conditions in the north, south, east, and west of the archipelago. Warm, nutrient-poor waters arrive from the northeast, particularly between January and March. Cold, nutrient-rich waters arrive from the southeastern Chile-Peru current and from the east, the Cromwell countercurrent, a deepwater cold current that upwells when it hits the Galapagos platform. These currents result in five different marine areas with distinctive oceanographic and biological characteristics.

The Galapagos archipolago has 1,118.5 miles (1,000 kilometers) of coastline and the Marine Reserve covers 85,749.2 square miles (138,000 square kilometers). This area includes intertidal areas, a relatively shallow platform of less than 650 feet (200 meters) deep, and the surrounding deep waters with depths from 0.6 to 2.5 miles (1 to 4 kilometers). Owing to the currents and these depth variations, the Galapagos Marine Reserve changes dramatically from one area to another and from one season to the next. In addition, unpredictable climatic events such as the El Niño Southern Oscillation (ENSO) phenomenon have substantial consequences for the islands. ENSO events can cause the failure of upwelling and the extension of warm, nutrient-poor surface water throughout the archipelago. Such radical alterations to the status-quo have inevitable knock-on consequences for the marine and terrestrial life of Galapagos.

The marine life is as fascinating as the terrestrial life, and while Darwin, unlike Beebe, was unable to explore the depths, he did note that the "bay swarmed with animals" when he first arrived.

A Longnosed Hawkfish, *Oxycirrhites typus*, hides cryptically amidst a colonial hydroid. Cousins Rock.

A young supermale of the Streamer
Hogfish, *Bodianus diplotaenia*, swims
amongst a school of Yellow-tailed
Surgeonfish, *Prionurus laticlavus*.
Isabela Island.

A Rainbow Runner, *Elagatis bipinnulata*,
is a fast, predatory, pelagic fish reaching
4 feet (1.3 meters) in length. Wolf Island.

A Marine Iguana leaves the sea bed to come
up for air after feeding for many minutes
on the bottom, grazing on marine algae.
Cabo Douglas, Fernandina Island.

Yellowtail Grunts, *Anistotrmus interruptus*. Wolf Island.

A tight school of Striped Chub,
Kyphosus analogus. Wolf Island.

Left: Bottlenose Dolphins, *Tursiops truncatus,* play in the calm, deep waters off Roca Redonda.

Bottom: An Elliot's Storm Petrel, *Oceanodroma gracilis galapagoensis*, patters the water looking for tiny food particles or oil droplets on the water's surface. San Cristobal Island.

A Galapagos Sea Lion swims down to play
with the photographer, scattering a school of
Black-striped salemas on the way.
Champion Islet, Floreana Island.

Top: A Galapagos Shark and a mixed
school of fish. Wolf Island.

Bottom: A Galapagos Penguin hunts Black-
striped Salemas off Bartolomé Island.

A large school of Scalloped
Hammerhead Sharks, *Sphyrna
lewini*, cruises at the limit of the
photographerís visibility, in
mid-water around Darwin Island.

A Whale Shark, *Rhincodon typus*, the largest fish in the world, is relatively common to see around Wolf and Darwin Islands. They grow to 49 feet (15 meters) in length, but are harmless plankton feeders. This one carries the ultrasonic tag, visible behind the dorsal fin, which was attached as in the photo on page 46 in the second half of the book. Several remoras, or suckerfish, can also be seen hanging on to the tail for a free ride. Wolf Island.

An adult supermale
Streamer Hogfish
off Gardner Island.
Española Island.

A mixed group of fish including Dusky Chub, *Girella freminvillei*, takes cover in response to a passing Sea Lion. Bartolomé Island.

Sea Lions play with the photographer
and each other. Gardner Islet,
Floreana Island.

A Spotted Eagle Ray, *Aetobatus narinari,*
glides effortlessly through the water.
Darwin Island.

A bull Galapagos Sea Lion patrols his territory, ascertaining the potential threat of the intruder. Champion Islet, Floreana Island.

Left: A female Galapagos Sea Lion barrel-rolls directly towards the photographer, only to swerve away at the last possible minute in a form of Sea Lion play. Champion Islet, Floreana Island.

Right: A bull Galapagos Fur Seal, likewise, inspects the intruder. Wolf Island.

A squadron of Golden Cow-nosed Rays, *Rhinoptera steindachneri*, swims in tight formation towards the mangroves and the inner lagoons of Caleta Tortuga Negra, Santa Cruz Island.

Bottlenose Dolphins enjoy riding the pressure wave, surfing at the bow of a tourist vessel in open water.

A particularly clean Green Turtle hangs in mid-water, watching the photographer. Santiago Island.

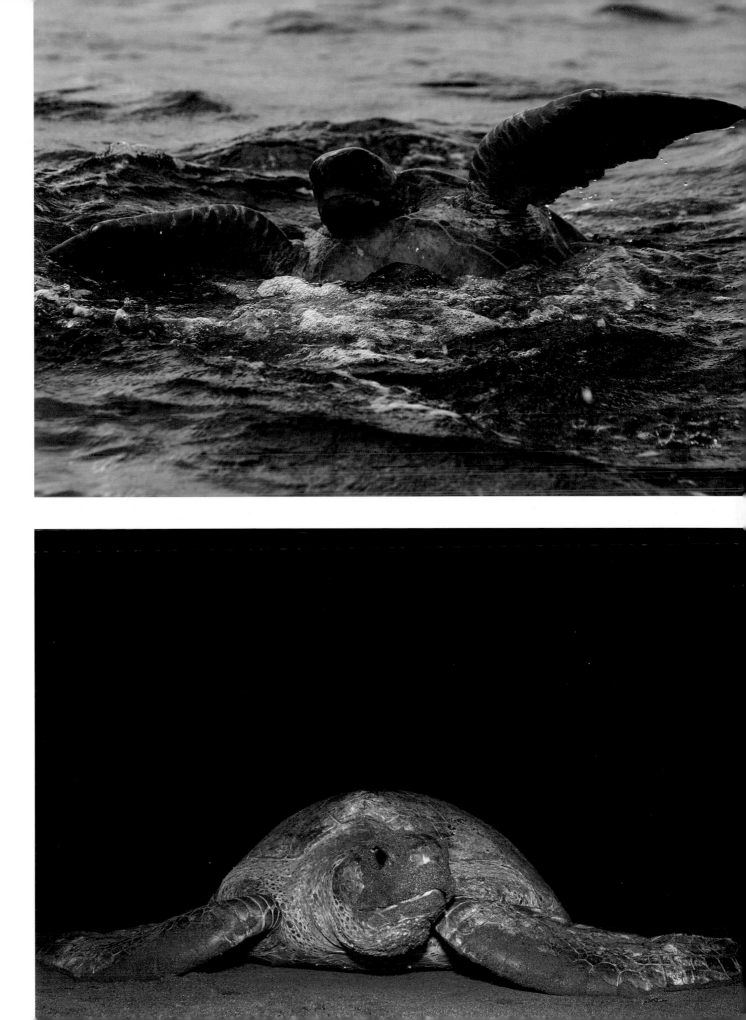

Top: A mating frenzy leaves this male Green Turtle partly out of the water. Santiago Island.

Bottom: A female Green Turtle returns to the sea at night after spending nearly two hours ashore, beyond the high tide mark, in the Herculeon effort of laying her eggs. Santiago Island.

A male Bluechin Parrotfish, *Scarus ghobban*, swims through a cave off Wolf Island. This is the most common parrotfish in the Galapagos.

The Moorish Idol, *Zanclus cornutus*, is a fish more often associated with more tropical climes, yet in Galapagos can paradoxically be found swimming with penguins. Wolf Island.

A Green Turtle throws its head back to breathe at the surface of a bay on Fernandina Island. Galapagos is an important breeding area for Green Turtles, with an estimated 1000-2000 females per year laying eggs.

A large adult bull Orca, *Orcinus orca*, characterized by a 5 foot (1.5 meter)-high, erect dorsal fin, patrols the waters hunting for anything from sea lions and fur seals to sharks and rays.

153

The shy Guineafowl Pufferfish, *Arothron meleagris*, is common throughout the entire archipelago, displaying two distinct color phases - the normal black with white spots and the much rarer golden phase. Both Wolf Island.

Yellowtail Mullet, *Mugil rammelsberi*, are common throughout the archipelago and can often be seen from shore as they break the water surface while feeding on plankton and floating debris. Wolf Island.

Above: The imposing silhouette of a huge Whale
Shark, the size of a bus, darkens the sky as it passes
over the photographer. Wolf Island.

Right: A Galapagos Shark patrolling off Wolf Island.

A pair of Blue-footed Boobies courting.
Punta Cevallos, Española Island.

"The natural history of these islands is **eminently curious,** *and well deserves attention."*

Darwin, C.R., 1845, Journal of Researches

Darwin was in the Galapagos for only five weeks. However, during this short time, he was not idle, but documented variation and relatedness of species, recorded aspects of animal behavior, and worked extensively studying the geology. He particularly noted that many species were "endemic" to the islands, or found only there and nowhere else, but that they were also similar to species he had seen on the South American continent. In addition, he incorporated many anecdotes on the behavior of marine iguanas, tortoises, land iguanas, hawks, and finches into his writings.

The role of protected areas, worldwide, is to maintain behavioral, ecological, and evolutionary processes. The Galapagos is no exception – ensuring continuity of critical biological processes is one of the key reasons why it was designated a protected area and why it has been recognized as a World Heritage Site. The Galapagos has contributed to our global understanding of animal behavior, thanks to studies on a wide range of species, including long-term studies on the albatross, boobies, finches, hawks, gulls, lava lizards, iguanas, and tortoises, to name but a few.

The Galapagos offers the opportunity for visitors to see these behaviors in action. Here, we capture some of the more common displays that also contribute to the "eminently curious" nature of the Galapagos.

A pair of Waved Albatross seem to
be celebrating their new egg during
a change-over of incubation duty.
Punta Suárez, Española Island.

A pair of Galapagos Flightless Cormorants prepare to change nest duty. Muñeco, Isabela Island.

Two Giant Tortoises in a show of dominance.
Accompanied by a threatening gape, the
dominant animal is the one who can stand the
tallest. Alcedo Volcano, Isabela Island.

Two large male Marine Iguanas push and shove in a fight over dominance. With raised scales on the top of their heads that tend to interlock, rather like a deer's antlers, he who pushes hardest wins. Punta Espinoza, Fernandina Island.

Left: On the remote island of Wolf, in the north of the archipelago, the population of Sharp-beaked Ground Finches, *Geospiza difficilis*, has learned to peck at the elbows and cloacas of the Nazca Boobies sufficiently hard to draw blood, which they then drink. Hence, their alternative name of Vampire Finches.

Above: Nazca Boobies preen one another on Española Island, while another bird feeds a chick.

Left: Two pairs of Giant Tortoises mate at the bottom of Alcedo Volcano crater. The rhythmic grunts accompanying the effort, along with the thumping of carapaces, can be heard over relatively long distances. Apart from a sharp hiss as air is expelled when a tortoise abruptly retracts into his shell, these are the only sounds made by the tortoises.

Top: Giant Tortoises, although not considered social, do congregate in muddy wallows to spend the night, a behavior which helps to maintain their body temperature. Alcedo Volcano, Isabela Island.

A male Magnificent Frigatebird, *Fregata magnificens*, flies with his pouch inflated back to his roost on the west coast of Isabela Island. It can take twenty minutes or more to fully inflate the pouch, which is used to attract a mate.

A male Great Frigatebird, *Fregata minor ridgwayi*, seems to have successfully attracted the attention of a female who has landed close by. Punta Cevallos, Española Island.

A Short-eared Owl, *Asio flammeus galapagoensis*, is most readily seen on Tower Island, where it has become diurnal due to the absence of the more dominant Galapagos Hawk on the Island. On Tower, it feeds predominantly on Storm Petrels that it pulls out of their nesting burrows.

Despite the rarity of the Galapagos Hawk, most visitors to the archipelago should be lucky enough to see one. Here, a male has brought a decapitated Lava Lizard to the female who is brooding a single chick that hunkered down out of danger on the male's approach. Cerro Cowan, Santiago Island.

A Greater Flamingo leaves a muddy
path through the shallow water of
the salty lake while feeding. Punta
Cormorant, Floreana Island.

A newly hatched Green Turtle braves the long expanse of open sand to reach the relative sanctuary of the sea. It did not make it! A Lava Gull was quick to spot the movement and swallowed the turtle whole. Tortuga Bay, Santa Cruz Island.

Within a few minutes, one individual Opuntia Cactus flower attracted a Sulphur Butterfly, *Phoebis sennae marcellina*, and an endemic female Carpenter Bee, *Xylocopa darwini*. Both insects, apart from drinking the nectar, will also pollinate the flower. The bee can be seen already covered in pollen from another plant. Alcedo Volcano, Isabela Island.

The Silver Argiope Spider, *Argiope argentata*, is a commonly seen, though largely overlooked, web-building spider. It sits in the center of its web, where its silver and black body is almost reminiscent of a bird dropping – a characteristic which perhaps helps to attract flies to its trap. Puerto Ayora, Santa Cruz Island.

A Galapagos Sea Lion scratches its back on the sea bed.
Gardner Islet, Floreana Island.

A Bottlenose Dolphin swims upside down, showing off, with a Creole Fish, *Piranhas colonus*, that it has just caught, in its mouth. Wolf Island.

178

A young Sea Lion quizzically
approaches a tourist to learn more
about her smell. Gardner Bay,
Española Island.

"I will conclude my description of the natural history of these islands by giving an account of the **extreme tameness** *of the birds. . . . It would appear that the birds of this archipelago, not having as yet learnt that man is a more dangerous animal than the tortoise or the Amblyrhynchus, disregard him, in the same manner as in England shy birds... disregard the cows and horses grazing in our fields."*

Darwin, C.R., 1845, *Journal of Researches*

It is impossible to visit the Galapagos without noticing the tameness of the animals in the islands. Darwin focused his discussion about tameness on the birds, but his comments apply equally to the majority of other species, including the sharks. Darwin allocated quite some time to trying to understand this peculiar phenomenon. He noted that the lack of reaction was not because these species were not wary of predators, but because they did not seem to appreciate that humans might pose a threat. We now understand that tameness is a characteristic of island species, and that this results from the absence of large predators on islands.

The apparent lack of fear has two results. The first is that many animals do not react adversely to visitors. The second consequence is, however, not positive: native animals find themselves easy prey for introduced predators such as pigs, rats, cats, and dogs. Darwin described the "extreme tameness" of Galapagos animals, but he also noted that they had not learned that "man is a more dangerous animal."

Fishermen throw scraps to Brown Pelicans
in Puerto Ayora, Santa Cruz Island.

Totally unafraid, juvenile Brown Pelicans hover in expectation of a free tidbit. Pelican Bay, Puerto Ayora, Santa Cruz Island.

Giant Tortoises lumber through the
campsite on the crater floor of Alcedo
Volcano, to see what is new in the area.
Isabela Island.

Domestic cows mix freely with wild
Giant Tortoises in the agricultural zone
of the highlands of Santa Cruz Island.

Completely oblivious to human presence,
Marine Iguanas continue with their business
of warming up in the sun, in preparation for
the day's activity. Fernandina Island.

Even while preparing lunch, fishermen and a little girl are surrounded by curious wildlife. Puerto Ayora, Santa Cruz Island.

Simply leaving a camera on the ground while photographing elsewhere is enough to attract the attention of the eminently curious wildlife. Punta Cevallos, Española Island.

Different perspectives. Española Island.

188

A Sea Lion, acting more like a domestic dog than a wild animal, nuzzles up to a fisherman, hoping for a free meal. Puerto Ayora, Santa Cruz Island.

A Marine Iguana takes a stroll past the gift shops along Charles Darwin Avenue. Puerto Ayora, Santa Cruz Island.

Visitors stroll past nonchalant Sea
Lions sleeping off a hard day. Gardner
Bay, Española Island.

Two students lying still on the beach were surprised when two young Sea Lions crawled over, lay on top of them and joined them in sleep. Of course, touching the animals is prohibited in Galapagos, but, in this case, the Sea Lions came to them, looking for thigmotactic contact – giving the girls a memory that will stay with them forever. Gardner Bay, Española Island.

*Stop reading here
if you don't wish to
see the 'other side
of the coin'.
If, however, you
would like to read
more about the islands
and to understand
how they have arrived
at where they are today,
then turn the book over
and start again.*

Blue-footed Booby.
Española Island.

*Galapagos is truly an extraordinary place
for an intimate encounter with nature.*